Crown N' Coke

Randy Randhawa

Instagram: @crown.n.coke

Dedicated

To All the Women whoever said No.

To All the Women whoever said Yes.

To All the Ladies who think about me without me knowing.

To All the Ladies who don't know that I think about them.

To the Hoes I Slammed.

To the Hoes I wish I had.

To the One I am in love with, but whom I haven't yet met.

To the One that may have been the One, but passed by already.

This is for you. You live in my Head Rent Free.

And Also To the Kids that got no Girls.

And To the Kids that think they got nothing to offer.

Can't forget about you guys.

I was, and in some ways still, one of You.

We Haven't Mixed Soda in Our Whiskey in Years.

The following are renditions of true events that occurred from my point of view. The following are viewpoints that each comprises a small bit of my soul. These are thoughts that have kept me up late at night questioning my own sanity; questioning everyone else's around me. Drug- Induced Alcoholic episodes are what set me off to the darkest recesses of my mind. I fell into this shit by accident and by no means am a formal writer. However, I have a story to tell, and at least a few of you want to hear it. If you have ever had a DM conversation with me as a fan you know that I appreciate you reading this "more than you know."

So What Did you Do?

You found one you liked, but she wasn't down in the end.

.

So what did you do?

.

Before you said fuck it you sent "one last text" for the third time. No response.

.

So what did you do?

.

Dejected, You called that girl that usually comes through. She wasn't the best looking or anything, but for times like this, didn't matter. Only you realized you're also just her thing on the side and she's with her real man tonight.

.

So what did you do?

.

Still kinda early so you dust off tinder. Buy a boost and let it fly. No matches you find attractive, and the ones you do either unmatch or didn't respond or live on the island.

.

So what did you do?

.

Went to the bathroom. Two pumps of Jergen and one of my favorite scenes. I'm not here for something new tonight, I'm here for comfort.

.

And then what did you do?

.

Shot millions of potential souls into the sink. Went to Sleep. Fin

Parents in India

16, a ripe age. Full of hormones, full of hope, full of angst.

.

From a time when porn was just a 30 second clip that you played on repeat via windows media player. These are the days of 2 times a day.

.

Both your parents are in India. They have been for a week now. They will be back in 2 weeks.

.

You've been eating nothing but frozen pizzas, chicken strips and sandwiches that your neighbour aunti makes you because your parents told her to look out for you.

.

You go to school. Not a care in the world. You think you have plenty of time alone and you take it for granted.

.

Few days pass. Weekend is here before you know it. Just yesterday you had 2 weeks left. Now your parents will be home in 3 days.

.

You gotta make something happen. Us brown kids rarely get opportunities where both parents leave the house.

.

That girl that you primarily speak to is your one shot to try and get some action in a place beyond a park, or a movie theater, or a bathroom stall during a high school dance.

.

This is your shot to lose your V card and not have to watch those trailers again. Atleast for a night.

.

She seems hesitant though. You pitch it to her at recess and lunch. Still no straight answer.

.

On the walk home from school she finally agrees. But I feel like I've almost forced her into it. However she says she has to go home first and do her homework and then sneak out at night.

•

You're naïve and you accept that to be the truth.

•

You still have a quarter of an Absolut vodka bottle left from your older brother's booze stash. Should be enough.

•

You're texting back and forth. You're not really doubling down on the hangout. You want to assume the sale, and if you keep bringing it up you'll seem insecure.

•

Right before 10:00 pm you message her if she still plans on coming over.

•

This is when you stop getting a reply.

•

You stay up until 11:30 before you get back to your trailers.

•

You wake up the next morning to see that text "oh sorry I fell asleep."

•

Look on the bright side, she lied but it wasn't to see another guy. She was just Brown. She bitched out.

•

Your parents come home a couple days later. They ask you how you were.

•

You wasted a golden opportunity. But this is just the beginning of lessons to be learned.

Just Wanted to Get Laid

(Screw-Faced) This is how I looked on the inside listening to your self-righteous bullshit on our first couple of dates. On the outside, though, I smiled. You had a fat ass and it had been a few months for me since the last time I slammed. Swiping for love has its downsides.

.

I just wanted to get Laid.

.

So I told you everything you wanted to hear. Laughed at your jokes. Agreed with your views on how suppressed you truly were. Agreed that your parents never actually ever supported you, with your $2000 Louis bag and your new Mercedes that one couldn't afford on a student budget. I agreed that your life was difficult.

.

I just wanted to get Laid.

.

I think the worst thing about this is that you knew I was full of shit. You saw in my eyes that I couldn't care less, and yet you projected that image onto me of a guy you could go on a while with, at the least. Someone you could alleviate that feeling of loneliness with. Someone you could tell your other friends in relationships that you had found a decent guy. But you knew...And As for me?

.

I just wanted to get Laid.

.

So after a few pipes, our flame had fizzled. I became more distant. And that was it. And you came to the conclusion that you had come to so many times before, "all men are trash."

.

Oh well. The show goes on, and the world continues to spin.

One Friday Night

Friday night, I saw my phone flash around 1:30 with "hey what's up" while the boys were at my place. We were wrapping up anyways but I would have ignored your text and went to sleep. I assumed you'd be drunk and just wanted to vent. It wasn't until that one right after "are you still awake" that you had my attention. That 1 minute follow-up in between texts revealed everything I needed to know about what you were looking for tonight.

.

I tell the boys I'm going to sleep, kick them out, and ask how far away you are. You say 25 minutes. You've called me twice since then so I know this must be serious. Your current man must have just been agreeing with you that your life was difficult, and he must have gotten what he wanted either yesterday or the day before. A classic move, but she does not know yet.

.

At 23 she's a young woman. She does not understand men yet.

.

I go to the washroom, beards a little rough and so is the chest, but passable. I look downstairs, about 3-4 days overdue for a groom, but still passable. This is not our first time where I need to make the best impression.

.

She comes over. She's sad. She's drunk. She's something else. Asks me if the white girl is present. Me and that bitch do not get along, but yes she is here. She gets intimate with her while I pour another drink and watch. I'm 8 deep, call it 12.

.

I don't ask too many questions about why and what happened, tonight is not the night. Our moments of passion are routine except that she asked me to focus on just her for some extra time.

.

I oblige. I'm empty on the inside, but I'm not a monster.

She lays in my arms and tells me she wants to stay over. Tells me she wants to pretend it's real, if only for the night.

.

And I'm going to let her.

.

She wants to live in that fantasy. Who am I to shatter that?

.

Who am I to send her back to that shit-hole we call reality anyways?

19 Year Old Randy

19 year old Randy. Fist for a Joora. A night out to the club is planned with the boys.

.

Pre-drink in an alley off Granville Street. 26 split 3 ways.

.

$20 to skip a 10 person line. We think we're too cool to wait with these heathens.

.

Head to the bar, need another drink before You talk to any girls. And then you have another.

.

You been laid a few times before, but something about the energy here seems hostile. Like they can see through your thin veil of confidence right to the nothingness of your soul. An uncomfortable feeling. You need another drink.

.

First approach, hot Apni, probably in her 20s. A lump in your throat. You take a deep breath. You take that first step forward. Before you even speak "EWWW GIANI."

.

Her words are daggers that cut you deeply with that one. That one sends you back to that insecure 14 year old place when you thought girls weren't down with you just because you were a Singh. Years later you would understand that was just a nonsense veil of excuses for you own lack of confidence, but tonight is not years later.

.

That one sets you off in a bad spin, like a bong rip after a long night of drinking. That one is going to cling to you for the rest of the night, maybe even the morning after.

.

You turn around with nothing to say. You won't even mouth her off. At this moment you are nothing. You need another drink.

.

What's worse is that your two friends have begun chopping it up with some girls. They go dance. You watch them have a good time from a distance.

.

You do anything to pass the time. Get another drink. Go to the washroom. Go outside for some fresh air.

.

It's only been 10 minutes.

.

You go back in and try to navigate your way through the dance floor when she bumps into you. But instead of hostility she smiles, you smile back. You exchange pleasantries.

.

She's receptive. She's hot. Atleast at the level of drunk of you are. It doesn't matter at this point.

.

You couldn't have been dancing longer than 20 seconds when you feel her being pulled away.

.

And guess who's doing the pulling? It's that bitch who cut me down. Crushes my soul and cock-blocks me in the same night.

.

The towel is thrown in. This will go down as a bad night. You go next door for a donair.

She Likes You

Maybe I'm the only one she sends those risqué snaps to. Even though those are posted on her story, the fact that she sends them to me personally must mean something right?

.

I mean I've only known her 2 weeks. We went out that one time and she picked the most expensive steakhouse in the city. She ordered a full meal and didn't eat much but maybe she wasn't hungry. Fancy places can have that effect on people.

.

The text convos have been going decent enough. I think we're really creating a strong connection.

.

Although she does often go MIA for hours on end and maybe even a day or two at a time. Only to return with a "omg I'm so sorry I've just really forgot to text back and I've been so busy!" This is usually when she needs help with her homework. But turning to you is a sign that she likes you right?

.

I know she only took 2 courses this semester and doesn't have a job, but maybe those two courses are really stringent.

.

And what about those snaps when she's out for drinks slightly showing a man's hands?

.

Maybe that's how she studies and that guy is her study partner. Who am I to judge study techniques?

.

Although he does seem awfully close in the next one she sends. And his shirt is off. His smile is awfully big.

.

But maybe they're studying kinesiology or something to do with human Anatomy.

.

Don't overthink it. Don't overthink. You always do this and it has only lead to negative outcomes.

.

Plus positive mind leads to positive results, right? Right?

.

She likes you bud, even though she hasn't responded to your last 4 texts over various platforms, she likes you. Those messages aren't even saying delivered anymore. But I'm sure it's just a glitch.

.

She likes you.

Excuses

"You're gonna hate me but something came up."

·

"I'm feeling a little tired so I'm gonna have to cancel"

·

"I feel like I'm coming down with something."

·

"My grandma is in the hospital."

·

95% of the time, these excuses are bullshit.

·

Knowing this, we still respond with something along the lines of "no worries" or "let me know if you need something."

·

Wanna know why?

·

It's cuz you're a fucking pussy.

·

The person you long for is probably out with someone else. Worse yet, they're probably at home doing nothing but watch Netflix.

·

That's how insignificant you are to their lives. That's how little you mean. That They would rather stay at home and waste a day of their youth than to deal with your simp behavior and your googly eyes.

·

It hurts. And it should.

·

We've all been there, and there is no antidote to the momentarily shitty feeling. There is however, an antidote to the situation as a whole.

·

Sack up. Work out. Work hard. Improve yourself.

Otherwise you might just "accidentally" receive a FaceTime call from that one you like and see this sweaty singh thrusting.

Pagliacci

Man goes to doctor. Says he's feeling low.

.

He says life seems harsh and cruel.

.

Says he feels all alone in a threatening world where what lies ahead is vague and uncertain.

.

Says nothing makes any sense anymore.

.

Men are acting like bitches. Women are acting like dicks. People are turning on each other at something as small as an off-comment. No one seems solid anymore.

.

Says he's starting to wonder if his existence is even real. Wonders if everyone is just a blip in his imagination. Wonders if he's just a blip in everyone else's.

.

Says as he ages, instead of gaining clarity, reality just becomes more absurd.

.

Says the money came. So did the clothes, vacations, and women. Yet he stills feels empty.

.

Doctor turns to him, visibly shaken. Says there's a clown in town tonight named Randy Randhawa. Go watch him, that should cheer you up.

.

"But Doctor, I am Randy Randhawa."

.

#pagliacci

2 Weeks

She said I'm just like all the rest.

.

2 weeks ago she said I was different from the others.

She tells me that my chest is too hairy.

.

2 weeks ago she said that she loved it.

She says she can't imagine a woman who'd put up with me.

.

2 weeks ago she wondered how I wasn't taken already.

She told me that my dick is small.

.

2 weeks ago she said she was still sore from the last time.

She said she feels like throwing up every time she thinks of kissing me.

.

2 weeks ago she told me to spit in her mouth; I hesitated but did it anyway.

She calls me a loser giani who won't be able to pick up any bitches going forward.

.

2 weeks ago she felt insecure about things as meaningless as likes on a post.

.

She tells me that I'm not even that funny...

.

Now she's just being petty and hurtful.

Moral of the story: don't take what your current partner says about you too seriously on either end of the spectrum. Those words are only a reflection of how you make them feel in that moment.

The Same Fuck Up

You came off too needy and got canned before it ever really began.

•

Worst part is that you've made this rookie mistake time and time again, even though you now consider yourself a veteran. Some women just have the power to make you that nervous 16 year old kid again.

•

Believe this: the heart is much more stupid than your dick.

•

You thought you were doing the right things. Not making her wait too long for a text reply. Treating her with respect. Asking how her day was. Doing everything you could to make it seem to her that she was priority in your life. Sending that God awful "Good Morning" You even paused that bumble account because you didn't want it to seem like you were still searching.

•

They had you believe that those were the right things to do when you actually like a woman for a change.

•

What a fucking idiot you are.

•

Other women have messaged you first because you've treated them as an after-thought. They have longed for you in your absence. That is the blueprint that has had success time and time again, and yet you ignored it thinking that this was different.

•

What a fucking idiot you are indeed.

•

We all want what we can't have.

•

You feel shitty but you can't show weakness. You call the boys to have some fun. "Tonight, We're Getting Fucked Up."

.

Except, tonight you don't have fun. You just get fucked. Too fucked. To the point that you're going to send a few texts to the flings of summer's past, and maybe even some nice girls. These won't be met with a positive response. In an inebriated state of mind, You don't give a shit. Regret won't settle in the next morning. But you live for the now.

.

You meet a couple of girls and get their numbers but have this all too familiar feeling that you won't get a reply in the morning. They're only here for Crown n' Coke.

.

And these days these girls aren't talking about soda either.

Growth

You already did everything you could think of.

.

You oiled her ass for 15 minutes.

.

You had her sit on your face until you ran out of air.

.

You did double windmills pounding from behind in succession until she told you to chill.

.

You wore her dad's pugg while you got domes.

.

You turned her from a non-swallower to a swallower... I don't even know why we as men enjoy that.

.

You went to the deepest recesses of your mind based on the years of porn you watched.

.

Something shifted.

.

This situation is not going anywhere.

.

There's nothing here beyond sex.

.

But because sex is taken care of in life, you've stopped chasing greener pastures.

.

You've gotten lazy. You've gotten stagnant.

.

You need to make that call, and tell her that this is a non-growth situation.

.

Not having sex forces a man to adjust his life.

.

He begins to workout, he begins to make improvements.

.

So I made that call. Telling her I need space. Telling her I can't continue to see her.

.

She was not impressed.

.

She turned from the sweetest girl into a horrible cunt, for lack of a better term.

.

It's my fault. But that's ok.

.

I needed growth.

The Lump

Should have been blissful times.

•

You were getting steady sex from 2 girls. At 19, you should have been in Heaven.

•

Except you were not in Heaven. You were in Hell.

•

This uneasy feeling clouded every part of your day. You noticed this feeling in the morning after your last escapade.

•

You had this itch. You had this irritation. You had this Lump.

•

But you used a rubber, except when getting domes. But who the fuck does that anyways?

•

I mean I knew one of these girls didn't have the best rep, but to give me something other than pussy was never part of the agreement. This was never on my radar of expected outcomes.

•

I freaked out, this was my first run in. And unfortunately I did what every scared kid does when they're mind runs wild. I Googled my Symptoms.

•

So now here I am freaking the fuck out. I make an appointment to see my general practitioner.

•

He's a guy. And for some reason I had no issue showing a guy my cock. He looks at it and refers me to the sex clinic.

•

There' a lump in my throat now too.

•

I pick a number at the clinic, I wait for an eternity and my name is called. I am told to pee in a cup and then wait in a room.

•

To my surprise, this doctor is a very attractive lady. She's probably in her 30's. Realistically, she's good enough looking that I'd let her give me this Lump.

•

She asks me what happens and tells me to get undressed; it's like every low-budget porno, except it is not that at all.

•

She says she'll be back in a minute and needs to grab a pen or clipboard... I can't remember.

•

What I do remember is being self-conscious about my size. Now if a woman sees me hard, and in all my glory, I do not mind at all. But all brown men would agree that when flaccid, we are very unimpressive.

•

Her leaving the room gives me the perfect time to get a few strokes in to at least have a respectable chub.

•

"Think about the hottest scenes, COME ON!!!" you give yourself a few pulls.

•

You're almost at a good level when she walks back in and catches you in whatever the fuck it is that you look like you're doing.

•

The energy in the room is fleeting. She looks down, and gives you some great news, although it seems that she is flushing pink and eager to leave the room in the wake of seeing you in a compromising position. She says it just looks like irritation.

•

The test results come back a week or so later.

•

Negative.

.

And since then I take a Sex Test every year.

.

One of the only moments I'm proud to be Negative every time.

A Bleak, Beautiful, Life.

You decided after date 2 that this wasn't going to work out long term. She has some interesting things to say and tickled your fancy in terms of looks but your differences were not the good kind.

.

However, she was rather progressive on her stance on free sex. A square would call her a ho. But I'm no square.

.

The bar was open. And when you don't know how long it'll take you to find the next one if this place were to go under, you drink till you puke. Then you drink some more.

.

And then a month and a half later she spoke those dreadful words, "so what are we?"

.

You decide you're not scummy enough to tell her you want to be an item just so you can maintain the steady lay. Sometimes you wish you were.

.

You synthesize a feeling of sympathy. You say things like "we're better than a label" and "lets just see where this goes" and the good ole "I'm just not ready to fully commit, at the moment." That last one is gold, it keeps the bar open.

.

She's not an idiot. She just wants to hear it. She has dealt with much worse than you before. But she has nothing better on the burner either. You will both continue this charade until either one of you don't have to.

.

It's a bleak, beautiful life.

4am in the Bathroom

It's 4am

•

The back of my throat and sinuses are coated in a thin sheet of frost. The taste of aspirin hits the back of my tongue.

•

That weird level of drunk and high where I am fully confident that my Mr. Hyde is the voice of reason. He has been taking over a lot more lately.

•

Regardless, you snap back into the moment and notice that she is still going off on her tangent. She hasn't shut the fuck up for the last 5 minutes. Her jaw jacks. She Done too Much.

•

You reply periodically with "yeah I totally feel you on that." That is the more eloquent way of saying "that's crazy" in moments like this.

•

You two might be fucking. That much should be established. That decision was at least partially made the moment she decided to hop in the post-club limo for promise of more booze and drugs back at your buddy's place.

•

You are in a bathroom and she is all but fully unclothed. You still have your boxers on. You just feel weird being fully exposed and not have a hard on. Must be the Hind in You. We are Growers, Not Show-ers.

•

She continues to go off about how she cannot find a decent guy in this indecent city. A decent guy? Perhaps she means a Liar.

•

She is in a bathroom with a guy she didn't know 4 hours ago and at least a half hour cab ride away from her place.

A cab ride that "I am definitely not paying for," you assert to yourself.

.

"No fucking chance am I paying for that cab. GTFO." You get lost in the thought. You prepare your response for yet another false scenario that will likely never manifest itself in the physical realm.

.

Anyways, being indecent yourself, you can't tell her where the path to a "decent" guy is, but this definitely ain't it.

.

You give her the deadpan. The silence of this moment sounds like tinnitus. You prepare to move in 80% of the way, but she is quick to pull the trigger and meets you at your 40. Lips meet and that hand moves from your face to your crown.

.

Only a queen is allowed to touch this crown. And you my dear, are No Queen. I move her hand to where it needs to be. She Obliges. The rest is a blur. She is treated like No Queen.

That Time in the car

The Year is 2008. Grade 11. 2 weeks until the beginning of Summer. Papers have been turned in. Naturally I have begun to slack off.

.

Hanging out by the locker with the boys and making plans to skip the next block to go get beers. I have my older brother's ID and that uncle who doesn't check it at his local liquor store. I glance over my shoulder and see her pounce.

.

She gives me a smile and hug, a routine occurrence from her. She has her books in her hand but I can tell she has no interest in going to class. I've always sensed she was kinda down, but I couldn't be sure. Plus making a move in a setting other than a dance could be suicide if I got shut down. She's 2 years younger. The Baisti would be too much.

.

A moment of brilliance flashes up. Nervously I ask "How about you skip and we grab a bottle?" I speak in a tone that is almost half joking just in case she said no. I can see my boys scowling at me, seeing as how their plan has just fallen apart. They'll understand, as all 3 of us are still chasing that first lay.

.

She lights up, she agrees. Off we go. She stays in the car. I grab a Bottle of Hypnotiq. Her choice.

.

We sit in the car at a spot you know. I pour up. She begins to tell me intimate details about the woes of her life. I listen intently. I actually care. I give that gentle shoulder-boy attention. I think girls want a guy like that. I think that is the path to the pussy.

.

She bats her eyes. Moves in closer. Silences become more tense. And me? I'm starting to pussy out. I try to force myself to make a move but am frozen by that fear of

Baisti. I have heard stories from other girls about how a guy came onto them and they got shut down hard. Those men were the laughing stock. You participated in those laughs, so maybe your turn is next again. A familiar and unpleasant feeling.

.

"SHES RIGHT THERE YOU FUCKING VAG. MAKE THE FUCKING MOVE. YOU FUCKING PUSSY." But to no avail. You continue to sip your drink. The time has flown and it's time to get back for lunch.

.

We part ways, I'd imagine even she's thinking about big of a pussy I am. I see the boys. Embarrassed, I lie and tell them that I got a hand job. A reasonable and believable consolation.

.

I never did end up slamming her.

First Hang with a Future FWB

From my faint memory, I believe it was a super-like from me that brought us together. After a bit of a learning curve I found that super-liking the super hot girls never really worked out. There were plenty of fellas out there that needed to drink more water. Super-Likes worked better on the above average girls; ones that you could tell would gel well with you based on their bios, and were hot in unconventional ways. Much like yourself.

.

The moment you saw that notification, you knew which one you had matched with. Conversation was fluid and easy. She was down. Within a day of speaking you had made plans to hang out.

.

Wonderfully enough, she was ok with you coming over with a bottle of wine to watch a movie. Her parents were out of town.

.

Before going over you did a full groom. Beard, Chest, Pubes, Lower Back. You showered and brushed your teeth right before you left the house. First hang, you gotta make a positive impression.

.

You pulled up and you called, she met you at the door. A hug for now. You go directly to her TV room and the movie is on pause. A hindi movie, not really your style, but it doesn't matter anyways.

.

You take a glance at her. Cute face and slim body. Tits aren't the biggest, but you're more of an ass man anyways. And she has a good one. You will work with this. Gladly. Also helps that she is relatively pleasant to talk to.

.

The bottle of wine is opened. She tells you she is a light weight. You are the plane ready to land; she's that person on the runway waving you in with those light sticks.

About an hour goes by from sitting side by side, to her on your shoulder, to you spooning her on the couch, to you finally turning her over.

·

The make-out is passionate. You're stiff and head is covered in Pre. Your black undies will show the remnants of tonight, tomorrow.

·

She won't let you fuck tonight. But has made it more than clear that you're headed in that direction.

·

You bid her goodnight. Until next time. Call my boy for the post-game breakdown. For a split second, you think this could be something more.

The Establishment of the Scene

The Second hangout was scheduled a few days after the first. Based off previous experience, you felt that you would need to wine and dine this one for at least 3-4 dates.

.

You went out to a decent place. Dinner was nice, conversation flowed, the cheque came. You walked her back to her car, beat her to the car door and opened it for her. You're getting closer to the lay with that one. You bid her goodbye, not really anticipating anything really.

.

Slight makeout, and nothing more. But you're good, you've done good work. You are probably a date away from some domes. What's nice is that she's actually pleasant to be around.

.

Third hangout is scheduled. It's routine but you delve deeper into details of each others lives. The surface level stuff has begun to erode. You find out she has the same last name as you. That shuts down the possibility of anything more than sex coming from this.

.

Don't ask why. It just does.

.

An intense makeout proceeds. She strokes you over the jeans, you ask for head, she politely declines. You part ways again. "Next one" you tell yourself.

.

She grows a little distant for about a week. You wonder why, but stay cool. Girls do this kind of thing to see how you will react. A younger me would have lost my cool as I had in the past. But this is not a younger me.

.

You try to schedule the 4th hang, but she "wants to talk."

.

Fuck.

.

She wants to know whether or not you like her more than she does. You think it possibly could have been more, but that last name is a deal breaker.

•

Don't ask why. It just is.

•

You give the spiel of how you enjoy spending time together but like things the way they are. Casual. You leave the possibility of it growing into something fruitful.

•

She's not interested in the latter. She's interested in the casual. She invites you over. Makeup on. She's ready to fuck.

•

The scene is established.

The Scene Dies

You have been fucking for a month now, two times a week. Tuesdays and Thursdays her house is free. It's like clockwork. She's becoming more open minded to the shit you've seen in porn. And you've seen a lot of porn.

.

You two aren't going out for dinners or movies or anything. Everything is going pretty smooth. Jokes land, she warms you up food, and doesn't give you too hard a time about things you said.

.

You fill her voids. The ones in her heart, soul, and well... the other one.

.

You start to think you have it made. Free sex without commitment. You brag to your friends about this girl being different and how she doesn't want anything more. You gloat about how they just don't know how to establish these scenes.

.

What a Fucking Idiot you are. Your arrogance blinds you to a historical truth: "Men and Women can't just Fuck."

.

It starts going South when she asks you to accompany her to things like college formals and other stupid Indian fashion nights. She makes a stink about it when you decline.

.

I mean why the fuck would I go? I'm already slamming. And I don't care to meet her friends, much like she wouldn't care to meet mine. They drink coffee in libraries before exams. We drink whiskey in alleys before the club. We are cut from a different cloth.

.

She says hurtful things like I am a selfish fuck who only cares about sex. She also says I am emotionally damaged.

.

I take great offense to the first part, it's only partly the truth. The second part though she has bang on.

.

Naturally, my defense mechanisms go up. I retaliate and say some terrible things that I don't really mean. Showing weakness would make it seem like I'm folding. I can't have that. I hold my ground.

.

I soon find that I am also left holding my own dick. The scene erodes. It's over. Oh well, was fun while it lasted.

Is the Grass Greener?

It has been about a month and a half since you last got laid. Ok fine, 3 months. But you have been focusing on yourself, at least that's what you tell yourself and your close friends that ask how your girl situation is.

.

It's the start of Winter. There are less people looking to get cuffed up this time of year. Most of the good draft picks are already gone; the free agents available are the ones no one wants. There are a few Tom Brady's still ready to get drafted, but you are not Bill Belichick. At least not to them.

.

Porn is a good, but it's a side dish like French fries. And you can't just have French Fries.

.

To think just months ago you were flying high. A pick of 2 girls. One that was already putting out. The other, who was hotter and had the better personality, seemed to be paving that road for you.

.

You may have even dated her. In fact, you neglected the other one to focus more on her. Maybe too much focus. It didn't work out in the end. The other one did not like the idea of being put on the slow simmer.

.

They Both Jumped Ship. Left you a Captain without a Crew.

.

You have faced this cycle many times. Ride out this wave. The tides will shift.

.

But they haven't for a minute now. It's ok you still have your boys.

.

But you call them up, and remember that they are with their girlfriends. You call your cousins, they are with their wives.

.

You open a bottle of wine. You throw on a good movie.

.

Who needs them, right? You almost think you are feeling envious, but the color green doesn't consume your aura, just a thin coat of grey.

.

You wonder what its like to be in a ship. You wonder if the way you're living is the wrong one. You wonder how the fuck you got here.
And then you remember the glimpses of what a relationship was like.

.

You'd rather ride out the down tide.

.

Opens another Bottle of Wine

That Familiar Flame

You finally cave in. You return to that place you said you wouldn't go again. You said you found nothing of quality in that place.

•

You open the app store and find that familiar flame icon. (For iPhone users) you see that cloud with the arrow pointing down. Inciting that you have downloaded before. It stares at you condescendingly.

•

You enter the gates. You pick some of the same pictures again, but add a new one to make it fresh and exciting.

•

You find it so weird that out of the hundreds of pictures you have of yourself, they never seem suitable for dating apps.

•

Essentially the same type of bio again: Something witty that shows that you are not your typical.

•

Your profile is fresh again so it appears more to everyone swiping.

•

You find that most of your matches through this next endeavor are the same ones you weren't interested in the last time. You reconsider.

•

You shake it off and you finally match someone new. You regurgitate the aspects of your personality that were received positively, and you suppress what was met negatively.

•

She'll have to scratch the surface for those. Never fully reveal yourself.

•

A few good days of chit chat. But for whatever reason, things fizzle out and one of you stop replying.

•

"Maybe the app is glitching and my messages aren't getting through" The person on the receiving end of the no-reply thinks.

.

You say fuck it, once again. You buy that Gold Memebership for the month.

.

You spend $20 a month on dumber shit. May as well go towards finding love in a hopeless place. Or atleast someone who will dome me for brief period.

Letter to Young Randy

Hey Buddy. Yes you with the full patka. Yes you in Grade 8 Fresh into High School. Yes you with these chips on your shoulders that are self-predicated. I'm talking to you.

•

Don't let it get under your skin when they call you Giani. It's a form of Self-Hate. This is a generation where it is still acceptable. I know the tides shift a bit just a few years after, but you are in the thick of it. They say it, you tell them to stop. They still say it, you get angry. They still say it, you knuckle up.

•

Unfortunately puberty hasn't hit you yet, you're still soft. But you got heart kid. And funny thing about it is that this form of hate comes from your own people rather than the others.

•

Shake it off. Don't take disrespect. Move forward. You have that light in your eye that none of these people have. That light is eventually going to dim, but while you have it, run fast and run hard.

•

You think Girls are going to shut you down for no reason other than being a Singh. But truth be told, that is just a crutch you hold on to. We all have these. Fat guys, Short guys, Guys with bad skin, Poor Guys, etc. The truth is that you're just not assertive or confident, Plain and simple. Everything else is just an excuse.

•

You're too nice to these girls, a shoulder boy per se. You're "High-School Harman" in Monster by Inderveer Sodhi.

•

You don't have any answers to the questions you have. You think different from everyone else, but then again, you'll find that everyone feels that way.

•

Women are on the way pal. Just not yet. There are many other parts of yourself that you need to develop before you can achieve that potential.

.

The Saddest and Most Liberating part of this is that I still haven't hit that potential. There's still a long way to go. A blessing and a curse I guess.

.

Life gets way better here in the future, but it also gets worse. The worries you had back then aren't the ones I have today, but they are worries nonetheless.

.

But be cautious, things get uglier out here. They also get much more beautiful. I just hope you're ready for it. Because I definitely wasn't.

Preparation for a Hot Girl

Wake up with a little bit more pep in your step. You locked down that date with that hot girl. She gave you the run around a little bit, so this is all that much sweeter.

.

You take your primary shower right in the morning. You do all of your male grooming now so you're not in a rush right before the date. You take your time. Beard, chest, pubes, are all taken care of. Nails are cut so you have a few hours to overcome that God-awful freshly cut nail feeling. You gotta be loose. You gotta be comfortable.

.

You already know the fit you're wearing tonight. Something that says casual but jazzed up. Something that says I dress like this all the time. Jeans and a button-up, and your good shoes. It has to look effortless otherwise she'll know you're putting on that front.

.

You're going to take her to a nice place. Not somewhere you take the other runts. A place you don't frequent. However, you can't look like you haven't been there. So you go online to the website and familiarize yourself with the menu. You know what to order before you get there. You have prepared to spend 150-200. You withdraw cash just in case the debit or credit machine doesn't work.

.

You are reminded of an awful time... But anyways back to it.

.

You want to look like a man who is sure of himself. This girl is Fine. She's better than Fine.

.

A good time to send that "confirmation of the plan" text is 3 hours prior. That shows that you're not too needy, but you're also well prepared. Work goes by slow until that time.

.

Your pals all know about this girl too. The discussion is ongoing in the whatsapp groups. They wish you goodluck.

.

She confirms with 2 hours to spare. Moves the date back half hour. You say no worries.

.

You take your second shower. More of a quick rinse to expel the funk accumulated throughout the work day. Teeth are brushed.

.

You leave a tad bit early. You stop by the gas station to buy a pack of gum. You message her "just left, be there in 20" when you are 10 minutes away.

.

You pull up outside, give yourself a final look. You wait 5 minutes before you walk towards the restaurant. Gotta be a tad bit late. Shows dominance.

.

You walk in to the eternal abyss. Soul may not return the same.

Preparation for an Average Girl

You wake up without feeling of too much excitement. This girl is ok. You'll slam as long as she doesn't put you through the ringer too much. In a perfect world, one date should get you the lay, but this world is far from perfect.

·

You look at your beard, you shaved 4 days ago when you went out with that Hot Girl. You're fine. Same goes with your manscape.

·

She sends a confirmation text to you around noon. Shows that she's looking forward to it. I am a bit out of her league, so it only makes sense. I reply with "yeah might be a little late." She says "no worries."

·

The whatsapp discussions with my friends tell the story of how I am almost dreading going to this date. I couldn't really care less at the moment. Girls like this never cancel though.

·

Taking her to a taco place I sometimes go to, and I don't mean mezcal either (if you know you know). With drinks and tip you're looking at 50-60 dollars. Not bad. If it were up to me, we'd drink a couple of bottles of wine at her place, but it isn't up to me.

·

In terms of fit, you're wearing track pants and a good hoodie. Not a sloppy look, you still look fresh, but you do not care to look your best.

·

You don't take a mid-day shower right before the date. There's no need, the morning one was good enough. You brush your teeth right before. You still don't want to be known as a guy with dirty breath, regardless of the situation.

·

She messages you to ask if you left yet. You're not doing anything important. You're sitting around watching clips of Seinfeld on youtube. Ones that you've seen a dozen times before. You wait 10 minutes to reply. And you say you're leaving in 5. Gotta get one more clip in.

.

You drive over without an ounce of nervousness. No bullshit here. You arrive when you arrive. You walk in when you walk in.

.

You have this in the bag. Zero Doubt.

That Type

You can never really explain it.

·

Why that certain type of girl has that power over you.

·

Why she can bypass all the logic in your brain.

·

Why she can make you act like a clueless fucking idiot.

·

Why she can take that Cool Guy persona you've worked so hard to create and turn you into a blubbering fool whose heart skips a beat every time your phone pings.

·

Why you get flustered to find out it was just an e-mail notification or a text from one of your boys.

·

Why you put the phone in a different room and not look at it for a couple hours in hopes that she texts you back in that time. And when you look at it then and find nothing, why you go into that dark place.

·

Why she can make you feel anxious and useless all at the same time.

·

Why she makes you say stupid things that reveal the insecurity and other low value characteristics within you.

·

Why you start to believe that this uneasy feeling in the pit of your stomach is in response to the realization that those negative characteristics are the real you.

·

Unwanted. Unlovable. Unattractive. Unbearable.

·

For me it was always the excessively sexy and flirty type.

·

The type that makes your loins ache and your jaw clench just thinking about a night of passion with her.

·

More than anything you just wanted to prove to yourself that she wasn't as great as this spell she had cast over you.

.

But you never got that shot to prove it to yourself. You fucked it up every time. And you never learn your lesson with those types either.

.

Because You enjoy sedation. Because You enjoy the spell. The thrill of that chase and what it might taste like once you finally get to drink from that cup.

.

No. You can never really explain it.

You'd like me if you got to know the Real Me

I think all people at least at one point or another have had this thought in the aftermath of not getting that mutual appreciation from a male or female they admired.

•

That they'd like you if they got to know you. The real you. The Funny Person. The Sweet Person. The Open Person. That Person free of all self-consciousness and hindrance of ideas in their head.

•

If they got to know the folds of you that you hadn't yet revealed to anyone before them. Or maybe you had and that person rejected that real you. But I digress. Was it even the real you? Or Just a Version?

•

They'd like the real you instead of this polished bullshit version of yourself that you portray yourself as in public or even the person you post online. But then again, these are the choices you made to reveal of yourself. You wanted to promote this exact persona to attract a suitable mate or mates. You hope that someone would see beyond this and try to scratch the surface of what was underneath.

•

You want them to find the real you. But you are lost Beneath your Bullshit Persona. Beneath your Bullshit Ego. Beneath your Bullshit Ideas. Beneath your Bullshit Beliefs.

•

The Truth is that we're all so focused on ourselves that we don't really take the time to dig too deep into what the person isn't saying. We just look at what they are saying and formulate an opinion at that face value. Even worse, we assume intentions of what someone was trying to say without having a real grasp.

•

So maybe this person that you think would like you based on what you have interpreted of them may not be the reality at all.

.

Maybe the real them is what doesn't fuck with the real you at all.

.

And maybe that's why the real them doesn't Fuck the real you.

.

But you still think that they'd like you if they got to know the real you. And it is your constant crutch that they don't like you because they didn't take the time to get to know the real you.

.

So tell me, well don't tell me, tell yourself: Would you even be able to handle that someone rejected the Real You?

Second Go on The Ferris Wheel

Another one has bit the dust. Unfortunately you went out on 4 dates and didn't get past an over the jeans stroke. In this case, that left you with nothing more than underwear full of pre-cum.

.

You download that dating app again. You swipe and because your account is fresh again, you start matching decently frequent. Except they are the same ones you said no to last time.

.

But what's this?

.

It's that girl you had the solid scene with. She's back here as well. You don't waste much time.

.

Even though you unfollowed her after an ugly departure, you still remember her username. You send that DM. A screen shot of her on Tinder and a smirk emoji. It's kinda risky. She could shut you down pretty hard here and you'd have to take it on the chin.

.

She takes it well though. She's still down. Too much isn't wasted. You make plans quick. She's coming over.

.

That first night of Sex is something out of the movies. Passions run wild, she's gotten much better at everything. You wonder how when its only been a year. Regardless it doesn't matter.

.

Maybe things will be different this time. Maybe you can be friends and things won't get cloudy. And for a couple months, it doesn't.

.

Except this time it's you that has the issue. You've gotten complacent. You're getting lazy. You're not even going out to meet new people anymore. You go to work. You stay at home on weekends. You eat pizza and drink beer. You're still getting laid anytime you want.

.

You begin to feel yourself in a rut. You know with her this isn't going to go anywhere. Something needs to change, and you know what it is. It's her.

.

You're gonna kick yourself after this is done, you're not gonna have a steady supply of sex.

.

But then again, you went 17 years without it. What's a few weeks? Alright, a few months.

.

But you like change in your life or you don't feel progress.

.

You end it swiftly and abruptly. She doesn't take it too well. She says "it's fine." But those words hold a terrible meaning.

.

She acts like a bitch, and you lash out. This time it's done for good. At least I think.

Rolling My Eyes

On a date with this new girl. She's brown, but she needs to let you know about how progressive she is. She needs to let you know how damaged she is.

·

You've heard the same shit before, but you're hoping it is coming from a genuine place. You always like a woman who harbors a bit of darkness.

·

But to no avail. She's full of shit just like the last few.

·

She tells you about her bisexuality. Seems to be a new trend these days. You ask her how many females she been with.

·

She says none, but she's made out with a few.

·

For fucks sake, I've kissed more bros on the cheek than this girl has had hot dinners. And I've probably shared more beds with people of the same sex than her. I definitely don't consider myself bi. Though I have more claim to that throne than she does.

·

She listens to the weeknd and sings along to how she can't feel her face, yet she bitches me out for popping molly at concerts.

·

She dresses in all black and takes pictures that promote nothing but numbness. Yet her mother cuts her up a plate of fruit in the morning for her hangovers.

·

She claims that all her past relationships were toxic. She says she cut a lot of people out.

·

But if she's still unhappy, is it possible that she was the toxic one?

·

She'll read this and take it as a personal attack. Don't worry darling, there are 20 others that are feeling the same way.
.
Don't place too much importance on yourself.

Its Just Different

It's Just Different.

•

Having a Friend with Benefits as opposed to a real relationship.

•

With a relationship, the energy of sex lasts longer because there is love and intimacy exchanged.

•

When it comes to Fuck Buddies however, the initial raw intense pleasure soon subsides after slam number 4 or 5.

•

I don't know about women, but for men it begins to fall under the category of "routine."

•

Ladies, this is when you'll start to notice a man doing some weird shit. Like not weird as in bondage or getting pissed on or anything like that.

•

That's for the freaks.

•

But I mean weird shit like catching him flexing in the mirror and wagging his tongue while he pounds you doggy.

•

Or putting on a documentary about Scientology while you ride him; but he's staring at the TV.

•

Or having to "check a message" while you give him domes.

•

Here's a little secret: He's making a video while that's happening.

•

Don't panic. If he's not a total scumbag (and 90% of men aren't), he's not making that to send over whatsapp. That is something that could ruin a girl's life. And 90% of men do not do that.

But he does this because he is bored and needs to show his boys. If he's a gentleman, he won't send it. It travels fast. But it is saved on his phone somewhere. And he will show the boys on the next hangout.

·

Monsters you say? I mean maybe it is similar to how women talk about whether he went down on you that certain night or not. Or if he made you scream.

·

Or whether he went 2 or 3 rounds and didn't quit after 1 because he didn't feel like being selfish that night.

·

These are two different worlds that maybe we're not supposed to understand.

·

All I know is. It's Just Different.

Old Flames

You heard it here first.

.

Going back to old flames is not a sign of weakness, but a sign of necessity.

.

It states that I have nothing better to turn towards at the moment, so I will re-till the lands that have already bared fruit.

.

The Old Flame will laugh. She will gloat. She will tell her friends "Look who came crawling back."

.

But even in her moment of feeling a higher than normal self-worth. She knows the truth, but she believes her own.

.

And you let her. You succumb. You admit defeat.

.

It is a true sign of maturity to show weakness in order to gain strength.

.

You only need that one opportunity to show her what she has been missing.

.

You put on the performance of a lifetime. You take extra time on her.

.

There is a shift in her conscious where she does not agree with her ego anymore. She begins to think you are the man of her dreams, if only for a second.

.

And you play that part, until the next flame arises like a phoenix from ashes from unknown parts.

.

And then you leave this old flame.

.

You add fuel to a new fire.

You continue the cycle, while the old flame runs out of wax. Runs out of Wick.

Age

My cousin once stated a beautiful line that never left me.

.

"Bro, men age like wine. The Vag ages like milk."

.

That should tell you everything you need to know about your worth as a man if you ever feel temporarily unworthy.

.

Keep improving your mind, body, and soul. Everything else will take care of it self.

.

.

.

And Queen, there is something for you here. You are precious so long as you pride yourself on being more than arm candy. Improve yourself and be better in all facets. You too, will age like wine. You will age even better.

Summer 15'

Was the summer of 2015.

.

I met this girl at a bar we frequented. From the first get go I knew she was down to get fucked. Just gave off that energy. I didn't ask for her number, she told me to take it down.

.

Naturally, I assumed she was a slut. Not saying that is the right assumption, just an assumption I had made at the time.

.

And boy was I right.

.

Within 2-3 days, the text conversations had turn sexually charged.

.

"A throbbing hard covered in pre" is the best way I could describe how she made me feel over text.

.

Another day or so passed and she was sending me nudes. Via snap chat of course. That way you can tell if someone saved em in the convo.

.

We made plans to "hang out." She came over that weekend during the day.

.

But when she arrived she was playing games, something we call in our community "nakhre."

.

Said things like "oh I thought we're only gonna chill" and "just so you know we're not having sex."

.

Generally I agree with this whole consent stuff, but I could see through this.

.

Told her to cuddle up as we watched tv, she obliged. More Nakhre though.

.

Went for the makeout. More Nakhre. On the 3rd attempt she obliged.

.

Makeout turned to the unbuckling of my pants. More Nakhre. Eventually, she went down, she was unreal. She'd been watching too much porn, and had too much practice. I wasn't complaining.

.

During sex, she kept her shirt on, I suppose as a last line of justification to herself that she wasn't totally giving it up all the way.

.

We finished. She swallowed. We hung out for a bit.

.

"Omg I don't even know how that happened, I'm really not like that" with a mist in her eye.

.

I am not that smooth. You are just easy.

They Ain't Coming Through

We all know the look on your face.

.

You're 19, fresh out of the spring semester finals in college.

.

You went to Langara. You been in the Criminology program, and for some reason the girls in your classes ain't been so fly. So far anyways.

.

Not to worry though, homeboy goes to Kwantlen Surrey, he's in the nursing program, where all the girls go.

.

Your mind trails off and you wonder why you didn't go there, but tune back in when you hear him say that he's got two hotties down to come out tonight.

.

Buddy usually pumps it a bit, but hotties mean they're at least passable.

.

Anyways, he further delves deep and says they're down. I ask him to send some pics.

.

They're better than passable. And on top of that, the friend for me is a blonde Apni who looks kinda slutty.

.

My favorite. Well at least at this point in my young life.

.

Regardless, the plan is made for 8:30 tonight, we're gonna pre in buddy's media room (his rents are out of town), and then we're headed downtown.

.

You go home, trim the beard, SHAVE the pubes clean. At this point you think this is the key look.

.

Fresh fit picked out, grab some condoms from the 6 month old pack that's been in your drawer. They're still good.

•

You're on the way, you pick up a bottle. You arrive at buddy's place. It's 8:15. Just enough time to get a fat peg in.

•

You gotta be loose for when they arrive.

•

Greet buddy at the door, he's looking fresh af too. You pump each other up saying how if things go well, you will bring these chicks back and slam them.

•

8:45 hits and there's still no sign of them. We are 2 heavy drinks in.

•

A quick feeling of anxiety begins to creep up, but you wash it away with the good ole concept of "Indian Standard Time."

•

Ofcourse they're coming.

•

Buddy calls them, steps out of the room. They don't answer. 5 minutes pass, he gets the call back. Our deflated attitude is pumped up again.

•

But only momentarily.

•

He gets off the phone. Looks up at me dejected.

•

"Bro. They ain't coming through."

•

He sees that look on my face.

Canada Day

It's Canada Day

.

When you were younger this meant an extra day off of school where you played video games all day without changing out of your pajamas.

.

Now it represents a day where the entire city gets fucked up and girls seem looser.

.

I don't know which I liked better to be completely honest.

.

Regardless this past one was unreal.

.

Head to Yaletown, drinking started at 12pm. We're getting fucked.

.

You drink at a bar where you meet the waitress. She's hot, but not hot enough that you wouldn't give it a fair effort.

.

She seems kind of down, so much so that she comes and has a drink in between serving others.

.

She plays with her hair, bats her eyes, asks for the vial you keep especially for situations like this.

.

As a younger man you would assume these signs meant nothing, but you are not him anymore.

.

She has to work, you have to leave. You exchange numbers. She promises to text you at the end of her shift.

.

You don't really expect anything to be honest, but she was at least interested enough for you to finesse this into a date.

.

After a fog of drugs and alcohol you feel the vibration of your phone. It's close to 11pm. She messages for you to come to hers.

.

This never happens, but you act like its routine.

.

You meet her outside her building with a long and hard tongue kiss, a 90% of a hard in your pants, a tip covered in pre.

.

You go inside her place, sit on the couch as she goes to the washroom to freshen up the funk from a 8 hour shift. She also asks for your vial. You don't mind, you use this time to wipe your tip with your boxers.

.

Can't look too excited.

.

The rest of this is fucked. Sex includes her asking you to spit in her mouth. She chokes and slaps you while riding. You kinda like it.

.

The passion passes. You wake up with your pug raised 3 inches but still on. A few stray hairs amongst your forehead. Never a good sign.

.

You tell her you're leaving; she is nursing quite the hangover herself so she doesn't mind.

.

What a night.

The Key

In the city of Gotham in which we live. I have long been told the key to sex.

.

It is not Neg Theory. It is not some fancy line. It is not nice clothes and a nice car. A city where everyone has money, that shit doesn't matter.

.

In fact it is a substance that fits in a glass vial. The sexually liberated (sluts) can't get enough.

.

The normal women, the ones we want to marry after our lifetimes of debauchery, are not the ones who will give you sex after a night out.

.

No, this is saved for the sexually liberated (sluts).

.

Any night on the town that you have this magical substance, even if you yourself are not indulging, your chances of getting laid go up exponentially.

.

A young creative once asked me the secret to getting white girls.

.

Ironically enough, to get the White Girls... you need the white girl.

Post Sex Aftermath (Dark)

You just finished having sex in a hotel room.

.

You use hotels because currently you don't have an open house to bring girls to. And you're staying with your parents. And you're tired of having car sex.

.

You're a grown man for fucks sake.

.

Regardless, you used a full night for 2 hours of a good time.

.

You now stand awkwardly in the elevator. Normally it wouldn't be like this, but for a one-night type of thing I always felt weird.

.

I always filled the void of silence with "so what are you getting up to tomorrow." She knows it's just filler, so she replies with non-chalant answers.

.

You don't mind, you just don't want to feel awkward so you overcompensate for the silence.

.

An hour ago, you were the only two people on the planet. Now, again you are the only two people on the planet, but with much shittier energy.

.

I can barely make eye-contact with her. Post-Nut clarity will do that to you.

.

Sometimes you drive her home, music loud so you don't have to talk. But if you were fortunate enough that she took a cab, you drive in silence just longing to get home so you can take a good shower to wash away the funk.

.

You want to make a phone call to you best pal and tell him how it went, that usually alleviates this empty feeling.

He Doesn't answer. You continue to drive home in
Silence.

Post Sex Aftermath (Light)

You finally did it.

•

You wondered if you were going to close the deal with this one. And after date 4, it may have seemed like she wanted to BF you up before she let you in.

•

There wasn't much physical escalation in the dates preceding. Took you 3 dates to even kiss. 4 to get a decent makeout.

•

But by no means did you expect her to hop on you like a wild banshee after date 5. Did all those things to you that you did not expect based on the previous interactions.

•

But this passage is not about the wild sex.

•

It's about that phone call you make to your close boys after she is gone.

•

The excitement. The pump. The stroke from the bros. For that drive home, we are the rulers of all creation. The conquerors of all conquerors.

•

When they say a gentleman doesn't kiss and tell, that means to the whole world.

•

For me, first call is to my boys telling them that I got it in. It is expected. The same way that I receive those calls from them.

•

If as a female, this surprises you, you are clueless and need to open your eyes to the world around you. But if you are like most, you understand this is similar to your girl talk.

•

To live vicariously through our boys is all we know. All We Love.

Pointless

It's like taking a piss in a public washroom but having to use soap because there is someone at the sink right next to you.

.

Pointless

.

It's like trying to avoid eye-contact with someone from high school that you knew but don't really care to talk to, but then asking them what they're getting up to these days when you couldn't avoid them.

.

Pointless

.

It's like trying to cram 10 minutes before a mid-term that you should have studied 2 weeks for.

.

Pointless

.

It's like getting that 5 extra minutes of sleep in your car before you start your shift at work.

.

Pointless

.

It's like getting only a handjob from a girl when you know she can't do you like you can do yourself.

.

Pointless

.

And that's what I feel keeping up this charade is.

.

How we both know there is nothing here.

.

But how you have this faint hope that I might change my mind.

.

That I might be that guy that wakes up one day and all of a sudden loves you the way you loved me.

I'm Sorry. I am not that man. Not for You.

Good Girl Vs Gusti

The Good Girl is the one that is in school to be a Lawyer or Doctor or Pharmacist.

•

The Gusti makes money and could be any of those things above, but does coke on weekends, and molly monthly or even bi-weekly. Who the fuck is counting anymore these days?

•

The Good Girl puts you through the ringer and makes you take her out to fancy dinners. Something you gladly do if she's worth it.

•

The Gusti is fine with going for drinks at happy hour as long as you don't judge her for the white particles in her nose.

•

The Good Girl makes you wait at least 4 dates.

•

The Gusti is ready to go as long as you have a place, and you're marginally respectful.

•

The Good Girl barely takes your slightly above average cock past the tip while doming. Her strokes are out of rhythm.

•

The Gusti goes all the way down, coughs, spits, has tears coming out of her eyes, and moans like a fucking ghost. She asks for feedback. Constantly.

•

The Good Girl's legs lock when you're missionary preventing you from getting the good strokes in. Her back is not arched in doggy. That's the worst.

•

The Gusti makes you wish you had more dick to give. She grabs your ass and pulls you in. She makes you pull her hair, and slap her at intensities that you find extreme.

•

The Good Girl makes you pull out and finish in the jimmy.

.

The Gusti can't wait to swallow every drop.

.

I just want something in between.

The Love From Toronto

Game 5 Raptors playoffs.

.

A loss stings, but I am numb by the 10-12 drinks I have had.

.

Also, a fan of the Rap Gods Podcast has stayed in touch and told me to hit her up if I was ever in town.

.

I did. And she replied back quite quickly.

.

She has also been drinking. And from the incoherence of her sentences and spaces in between words, she's had a lot to drink.

.

My friends and I continue to drink until 1 am.

.

I give her the address to my hotel. She agrees to show up.

.

I run a quick shower and wait. Gotta stay Fresh.

.

She keeps me updated every 5 minutes, she is there within half hour.

.

Even in my drunken state, she is a notch below what I would consider passable.

.

But she is down. A groupie if you would.

.

I plow. You don't turn down free sex, especially on vacation, especially when they love you for a slice of who you are on camera. Even when you are a nobody in terms of relative "fame."

.

I send her on her way, she doesn't try to stay the night.

.

I shower again. I think about how a low-level podcast was able to get me free pussy from a Thousand Miles Away.

Thank You For the Love Toronto.

The Art of the Cock Pic

So you've gotten to a point with a Woman where the texts have gotten quite steamy.

•

She's telling you about the nasty things she wants do to you. You tell her about the nasty things you want to do to her.

•

She begins sending nudes. If she's any smart she sends them on Snapchat where you can tell if someone saved them.

•

They haven't figured out a way to stop someone from screen recording and pausing to screenshot on your own. But that's a story for another time.

•

But now she wants to see what you're packing, and maybe you're a bit nervous as to what she'll say.

•

Disclaimer: This is more a young man's game from 19-24. Don't send em before that, your cock isn't fully developed. Don't send em after that age, you're a grown man. Have some fuckin class.

•

Regardless, make sure you have a throbbing hard. Don't send no loose dick half-chubb bullshit, ESPECIALLY if you're a brown guy.

•

We are growers. Not Show-ers.

•

Next, lotion up a bit. The shine makes it look sick.

•

Make sure your shit is trimmed, no girl thinks "OMG I REALLY WANT TO SUCK HIS COCK AND PICK ALL THOSE PUBES OUT OF MY MOUTH."

•

Lay on your back and have your cock falling onto your stomach.

- Front Camera on. Skin down if you're not circumcised. That seems to be the best angle for size and aesthetic.

- Tighten the stomach. No one likes a FFG. No one likes a Fat Fuckin Gut.

- Take a few and find your fave. Flash on. And for fucks sake keep your face out.

- Keep in my if things end badly the girl will send this to her friends to roast you.

- So make sure it's a good one.

Lets Be Real

"I just don't know why guys are always sending me DM's."

.

Maybe its because you have an open profile and have most of your pictures up with your tits out.

.

"I just don't know why someone would send me a cock pic out of no where."

.

I agree it's pretty hasty and will probably never work, but maybe it's because you send every guy on your list a quick video of you putting on your jeans and trying to look hot.

.

"I just don't know why guys are always staring at me."

.

Well for one, you dressing like a harlot and looking hot is not for yourself contrary to your belief. In fact you wouldn't feel "empowered and sexy" if men weren't giving you those googly eyes in the first place.

.

I mean lets be real, is a thong or G-String more comfortable than granny panties?

.

Is taking 2 hours to do your hair and makeup making your life any easier?

.

Is buying a new dress that hugs every luscious curve of your body really good for your wallet when you have a hundred others?

.

No.

.

You do it because you like the attention so lets quit the bullshit.

.

Why can't we accept that? Why do we have to pretend?

Men do it too. It's the only reason we don't walk around in sweats all day.

But can we please drop the bullshit?

Or atleast stop posting your whorey shit and fat fucking ass all over the place for the world to see, just to have them captioned by inspirational and positive vibe mumbo jumbo.

"I would never" turned into "Fuck it" one faithful night.

•

"Never again" turned into "Fuck, fine just once more."

•

A bad night hit... you called buddy over and had some.

•

That turned into you "Fuck, may as well you're in Colombia."

•

That turned into "Ok, only on vacations."

•

That turned into "Wedding receptions too... and some of the days leading up." This was only when it was close boys.

•

All of a sudden you found yourself once a week during the summer.

•

That turned into special occasions throughout the year.

•

At one point, that turned into help to write this book.

•

•

•

And luckily, that's when you were able to catch yourself. Before it became a real problem. Before you started losing work. Before you started losing money. Before you started losing friends.

•

No judgment from me, but keep use to an absolute minimum. Avoid it entirely if you can.

•

If you continue to party in your later 20's to 30's you will probably come across it.

•

You are a recreational user at best, you are lucky. Some of your friends, not so much.

They can judge you if they wish. You don't care. The world has bigger problems.

The Park

For us Hinds, the Park has always been a special place.

.

For us it was the place to get drunk, fight with your best friends, and cry when you made up minutes after.

.

It was the place where we got our first handjobs. The place where we got our first blowjobs.

.

It was the place where 3 girls coming to hang out with 10 guys all of a sudden became a "Scene."

.

It was a place you lowered your standards because of the lack of available women. But you didn't feel shitty about it.

.

It was a place that you and your boy could call out two girls and have the best time with nothing more than a mickey of vodka mixed in two big slurpees.

.

It was the place that you tested your manhood vs some other guys at the park because someone started at you for a split second.

.

It was our Country Club.

.

But eventually, you get older and have places to drink all of a sudden. You stop going to the park as much. You start to drink in Garages and Basements or if you're more classy Clubs and Bars.

.

Don't get me wrong, these times are still good.

.

But nothing compares to the great times at the park. A place where boys became men. Girls became Women.

.

A place where we were the Rulers of the Universe.
.
...Until your parents called and it was time to come home.

I'm Happy For You

I see that you just got engaged. That ring looks nice. The photographer captured that moment well too. You look so happy.

.

I'm happy for you, I truly am. It warms my heart.

.

You deserve all the happiness this world and this man has to offer.

.

But events like this do make me ponder. They do make me wonder.

.

I sit. I reflect. I consider the other man's position.

.

For instance, Does your man know about all the things you did prior to this engagement?

.

Were you completely truthful with him?

.

Did you bare your entire soul to him, and did he accept all of your flaws?

.

Did he embrace your dark past so together the two of you could create a bright future?

.

Did he see all the dimness of your imperfections in a perfect light?

.

Did those numerous quotes about love you have on your feed hold any truth?

.

Did true love prevail in the end?

.

Or... did you omit a few things?

.

I won't bring up the rumors of what I heard from other guys. I'll just speak from my position.

And I'm not calling you a cheater, I have no right or proof to do that.

•

But Did you tell him about the night me and buddy partied with you and your girl at a crummy hotel? While he had her in the bedroom and I had you in the bathroom?

•

Did you tell him about the time you domed me while I drove, all while I was munching on a junior bacon cheeseburger from Wendy's?

•

Does he know about all the times I snuck you into my place?

•

Does he know about all the times you left my car windows foggy?

•

Does he know about the time you gave me head on the jungle gym that one summer night?

•

Does he know about the snapchats you sent "just to me?"

•

Will he ever know that, objectively, his future wife has been branded by the ugly term "slut?"

•

Regardless that's just me on another deep thought that leads no where positive. I think some things are better left unsaid.

•

I wish you best in your marriage. I truly do.

•

Hopefully you built this relationship on a foundation of trust and goodwill.

The One and the Other One

The One that you like has been giving you the run around for the last little bit.

·

The Other one that likes You messages you good morning every day.

·

However the One that you like has agreed to go out with you, but she's taking hours to respond to each text. Much like you do to the Other one.

·

The One you like said yes to the date, but hasn't made the details of when and where concrete. Never a good sign, but you stay positive.

·

The One you like makes your loins ache in a way that the Other one just doesn't anymore.

·

It's not that the Other one is unattractive, in fact not at all. But she's too available and is a dragon you have already slayed... many times. Never the best trait.

·

Regardless, you make plans with both knowing full well the One you like could easily say she's "just so tired and wouldn't be much fun 🫤🫤" before she cancels on you.

·

And if she is down, you could cancel on the Other one saying that you're "Starting to get sick and Don't want you to catch something."

·

Regardless, you wait. And you twiddle you're thumbs. And you hear a ping!

·

But, it's the Other one asking if you should pick her up or if she should drive... you hold off on that reply.

·

But it is starting to get close to the point where you have to make a game time decision. You can cancel on the

Other one with a 2 hour notice before the scheduled date.

.

It's a reasonable notice to cancel, and you are a reasonable man.

.

You may be a prick, but you're not a total cocksucker.

.

The One you like hasn't messaged yet. It's one hour before the game time decision. You can't call her either because you sent the last text asking for details. You'd seem too eager. Women hate eager. Much like men hate easy... at least after the first few slams.

.

With 5 minutes to go the One you like comes through with the message "8:30 sounds perfect! Here's my address..."

.

You cancel on the Other one. She is disappointed. You sense it in her voice. You get the feeling she knows what's up. You almost feel bad.

.

And then You remember how many times in the past this has been done to You.

.

So Fuck Off.

You Won't get that From Me

You said you'd know me for me, but then went around asking about me anyways.

.

Don't worry I heard.

.

I mean most of that shit isn't even true.

.

I do ok. I slam often enough, but they paint me as this guy that is just sex, drugs, and alcohol ALL the time. That's only once in a while. Recreational is more appropriate.

.

I don't mind though, it is in your nature. I am not surprised.

.

This lead to our eventual demise. You dumped me, I won't even bullshit like most men will and say it was mutual.

.

You canned me. Plain and simple.

.

I know I lashed out emotionally. I said some things that I probably shouldn't have.

.

But to tell you God's honest truth, I was kind of relieved.

.

I was battling in my mind for weeks before this. Maybe some of it bled out in our interactions and coupled with what you heard about my reputation.

.

You were a good quality woman. Marriage material as one would put it. Good career, Nice Girl, Good Family, Average Looking, and Sucks my Dick when I ask... when you were in the mood anyways.

.

I thought I almost found marriage material.

We've been brought up to have fun with hot girls but not marry them unless they check the other boxes first. The other boxes are more important. They hold more clout. I mean we're not wife-ing up Ogres or anything but, historically, the average ones are usually of the best quality.

•

It's all besides the point. I was wrong. Once again.

•

I'm not shook.

•

What surprises me though is that, like after every other relationship (major or minor), I have not called you in my Mr. Hyde State.

•

You have not gotten that druggy- drunk call from me at 3 am. Hell, given the right cocktail and emotional state of mind, I give those to people I don't even know that well.

•

No, you haven't gotten that from me.

•

And to be quite honest, you will not get that from me.

•

I mean I think about you sometimes, naturally. But not for a second am I willing to give one last ditch effort to make you believe that I miss you.

•

Because the more I think about it, I really don't.

•

Maybe I was never that down in the first place. Maybe I just thought you were the right fit given my stage in life. My environment played tricks, and I almost succumbed.

•

But God knew better. Maybe the devil had a bit to do with it as well.

.

No you won't have me fight for you. I apologize if you expected that, but that energy is better spent somewhere else.

.

I am meant for Greater. That's not necessarily Better.

Part 2

In all honesty, it was probably around poem 30 that I figured out that I couldn't keep these up forever without really pushing the envelope to a point of no return. The challenge I am facing is that many of the women that I am writing about are women that I am still cool with. The point of this book was never about shaming anyone or putting anyone down (unless you don't fuck with this direction, then I don't really care), these were just my thoughts on the situations that I had been involved in. They were my perspective. So the poems are coming to a slow. This will be my one and only book. Hopefully it kind of pops off so that I can tour 4-5 cities and do some live readings where we get fucked up and party afterwards. That was kind of the vision of what I had for all of this. Lets see how this all plays out. The following will be a few other thoughts that I have had. Things that keep me up. Things that make me say "Just stfu" whenever I am reading someone's bullshit post (I'm sure people say that about me). Most of you will not agree. This is not for most of you. This is for the First 50 copies

I sold. This is for everyone that bought it right afterwards. I didn't do this to make money, it was just to see who's with me. If you're reading a second edition, I appreciate that you hopped aboard. Enjoy.

Mental Health

Everywhere I fucking look these days, everyone is looking to support someone with a mental health issue. Oh, you can't get that dream job? It's because you didn't take care of your mental health. Oh, you can't talk to the boy or the girl that you like? It's because you have the mental health issue of anxiety.

We as a society have turned mental health into a crutch as to why we can't achieve certain things. The truth is that we all suffer from issues. Every single one of us. Let me fill you in on a little secret: The Real World does not give a fuck. The Real World demands results. It doesn't care if you need a day off or two to gather yourself. If you don't get results, you get replaced. Its that simple. I can't fucking stand this narrative that we have created that someone out there actually gives a shit. Everyone has their own problems to worry about.

Sack the fuck up. No one cares. Move Forward. Progress is all there is. Accept this truth now. You will be better off.

Soft World

I honestly feel that this world has gotten too soft. I have been part of the side that longed for more understanding and compassion. All that love and positivity once seemed like the brave new world.

Until I grew up. Until I saw the world for what it really was.

A world in which half the people don't care about your problems, and the other half of people are happy that you have them just so they have a measuring stick of shittiness of their own lives.

None of this matters. Who knows how long we are here? We are on an eternal chess board playing a game. A game that we should all play to win. The sad fact is that even your closest friends and family have their own issues to deal with that will take priority when it comes to you. That is unless they hope for their own salvation from sin by setting out to save others. For which that is a selfish reason unto itself. To take responsibility for another's life while we can't take reigns of our own is the ultimate sin.

Yet we commit that most readily.

Regardless, no one has your back. You have to have your own back. The cavalry isn't coming. You are the cavalry. Now take control of this shit and ride forward. Stop being a fucking pussy.

God

This New Age notion has often lead us to believe that we are the creators of our own universe. While I fully agree with this, we often forget that there is a Creator of these rules. We are the controllers of our own Chess board, but we still play the game of Chess. We still abide by the rules of the Creator.

A cab driver once told me in a drunken haze in a fruitful conversation about God, "Without God there are many rules without reward, but with God there are many rules and we reach a reward." To you, the reader, this might not sound like much. But re-read that 10-15 times before it settles in.

The Lord is the only thing that makes this reality sensible.

With God, all of reality makes sense.

Without God, none of reality makes sense.

Keep God in your heart, and move through this spiritual journey. For that is all there is. For that is all there will be.

The Devil

I like to assume that I am quite the man of God. But in all honesty it is the devil that influences my flesh so long as I am on this planet. I love to sin, plain and simple. I love booze and bitches. Occasionally, recreationally, I also like to add drugs into the mix. I unashamed to admit this because I believe no one should be ashamed of anything that they do. If you are ashamed and if you hide something, then don't do it.

Regardless, the devil plays a major part in all our lives. Notice how I will not capitalize his name much like I do with God. It's quite simply because that force does not deserve praise, but it does deserve respect in the sense that too much time with him will kill you. The devil can take you to some fun places. Places that God won't go. However, only through sin can we find solace. Only through bad can we find Good.

So dance with the devil. Go to those places you would not otherwise go. Sin is fun. But that is all it is.

Sin is just stimulation of the flesh, but you need it to make it through whatever the fuck this journey is.

Just don't dance too hard or become his pal. Make sure he's one of those friends that you're cool with but wouldn't tell him all your secrets. Make sure you keep him at arms bay. He's a cool guy but if you trust him, he will fuck you over. Make sure he's that friend that is your friend outside of the home and not one you invite in... Even if he knocks at the door like the many times he has knocked at mine.

Because once you invite him in... he may never leave.

Toxic

Lately I don't really understand this push by society that we need to cut off these "Toxic" people or "Toxic" situations. While I agree that you should not give much time to that which does not help you grow, I often find myself at a loss for the definition of toxic.

I recently touched base with an old friend (some girl I wanted to plow but never did). She told me about how she had to cut of these toxic people in her life. And how she now hung out with completely new people. I often wonder if she realizes that if it was possible that she was as toxic of a person to the others in that situation. I find that we never take responsibility for the fuck up that we committed, and instead we love to blame the other for being negative. I did not say that to her though because I wanted to fuck. Which I did. But that's a story for one of the poems.

The Point is People don't responsibility for themselves in this world anymore. What's worse is that society is constantly reaffirming this in our own little worlds. And I feel strongly about this now because I have gone through that transformation of being a victim into being someone who is in control of themselves barring a freak accident.

There are no Toxic people or Toxic Situations. Just situations that don't agree with you. Trim the fat and move on, but make sure you remember that you were part of this problem. Even if it is in the sense that you failed to recognize and allowed negative things to happen to you.

The New Rat Race

We often think because we are in this new age reality where we all chase our dreams and how we love what we do and we tell each other about it in our endless bullshit masquerading around as positivity and insight, that somehow we are more woke than the generations before us.

The truth is, the rules may have changed, but we are stuck in a deeper rat race than ever before.

Gone are the days when you can just work a 9-5 and live a decent life. Now all of a sudden we have to do something that "drives" us even though it does not provide any monetary value. While I agree that pursuing your passion is crucial to feeling alive, your creative projects need to be on the back burner while you focus on something that allows you to build wealth. How much will be different for everybody, but figure it out. Louis Bags ain't cheap.

Gone are the days where you took a vacation once every few years to a place a few hundred miles away. Now all of a sudden we have to "see the world." We have to go back-packing through Europe. We have to stay in hostels in Asia. We have to go to Bali. We need to do all these things to "learn about new cultures." While I agree that one does need to travel, I will point out that it is over-rated in the sense of "finding yourself." Honestly, it's just a big self dick-sucking contest where we compare how cultured the other person is based on how many foreign countries they have visited. What happened to the grass being the most green where you water it? Why do we feel less as people just because someone has not eaten ramen in Japan or fucked a hooker in the red light district Amsterdam.

Gone are the days where you can just be a regular Joe. A person who aims for normalcy is viewed as someone who is wasting their life.

And while we should all strive to fully maximize our potentials, we shouldn't make the ones aren't feel less as people. We shouldn't hold our noses in the air just because we choose to paint at night. We shouldn't have a stick up our ass just because hoes wanna fuck because

you write some bullshit insights that you some call

poetry.

The matrix is inescapable.

New Year New Me

I believe that the concept of "New Year, New Me" is one of the stupidest things in existence. What's worse is that being at the end of 2019, we are in this "New Decade, New Me." Like somehow a man-made holiday that signifies the rotation of the planet around the Sun will fix all your problems.

You don't grow year by year. You grow day by day. Time is just a bullshit construct made to me you feel like things will be better in the future. They will be, but that doesn't happen by magic. You have to constantly work towards goals to make any sort of better future.

We all have a million things we want to accomplish before our time is up. However, none of those things will happen until you get started on at least on of them TODAY.

There are no years, there is just time. And some of us have more than others. Some of us, including myself, have gotten a better roll of the dice than others. Point being, life isn't fair. But you still have to push and strive for everything in this life.

Stop your bullshit. Pick up your ass. Move Forward.

Things began to get really serious in regards to the spread of the Corona virus to the rest of the world while I was in Las Vegas. I was there for my oldest friend's bachelor party and had pre-planned an absolute AMAZING time to be had. I looked forward to this vacation for a couple of months.

We got there on the Wednesday night. Fuelled by alcohol and things you do with alcohol, we hit the town. Strip Club was the move. What a reckless time that was. Unloved ladies writhing upon our half chubs turned to throbbing hards, and taking dollar bills from our mouths into their panties. Not a care in the world. The Lords of all Creation.

Thursday Hits. News begins to break. Still we consider ourselves lucky. We were in Vegas for the last conceivable weekend that parties would commence. We were afraid of no cough.

Few hours pass. More alcohol. More things you do with alcohol. Texts from promoters saying pool and nightclubs are cancelled.

We still make the best of it, met some great people. All the women I meet are working girls. They all want some money even if you're not interested in sex. Time is money. If you ain't paying, someone else is.

Needless to say, not the best vacation I have ever had.

The point being, none of this shit is in our control. We only think we have been in control. We want things to go back to normal, but there was any normal to begin with. We were only given the rights that seemed like a good idea at the beginning.

Take a look at the world right now. Allo of our rights have essentially been taken from us. When things finally do begin to roll again, most of everything we had before will be given back. However, the governing structure will tighten the noose once again.

I don't mean to scare you with an Orwellian state of affairs. The truest lesson to maintain in all of this is to remain positive. Use this time to find yourself even further. Dig deeper. Enjoy nature. Read some books. Craft your old hobbies. Begin new ones.

I have no idea if CO-VID 19 will still be a thing once this book is out. It doesn't matter though. Count your blessings, and make sure once this whole thing has passed that you can say that you enjoyed these moments instead of being ridden by anxiety and worry.

Nothing really matters.

Beefs

This one is for that young brown going through a squabble or having been through a squabble that could potentially turn ugly. We are all Punjabi, we all have cousins or buddies who are a little grimey and if push comes to shove, guns are in place to settle a score.

However, unless you yourself are heaty, you got no business pursuing beefs and continuing this shit on once you are past the age of 20. No argument, no matter what is said (unless they talk about your mom), is worth you looking over your shoulder for even 1 second and feeling unsafe walking around your own neighborhood. That is to say that anyone at anytime can get caught slipping and have a car full of guys pull up on them.

I have been there. I have done that.

First one I can recall is when I was 15 and my thick-headedness cost me a friendship with an all round solid guy. A rift that would cause much greater issues down the road. The issue was completely my fault. I called my buddy's sister hot. When he called me out on the issue I was too stubborn to take responsibility and didn't want to look like a bitch. This resulted in a 1 vs 1 fight where I got my ass handed to me. I landed a few good shots, but had no idea how to throw hands. This lead me to my martial arts journey where I learned how to fuck up the taller and rangier man, but that's besides the point.

Main thing is that I lost a friendship, and the whole situation could have been avoided with a simple apology. Years later, he was able to accept my apology in a drunken haze at a mutual friend's wedding reception. I am grateful that I don't have to carry that burden with me any more.

We, as a collective crew, have had beef with another crew for over a decade now. It has proven to be the most pointless waste of time that one can encounter. The pattern goes like this: We see them out, they "look" at us, some jawing back and forth commences, few shoves, maybe some punches, maybe bottles thrown, and the following day one of either sides gets a phone call telling or saying how the other is "dead." I can speak from experience as someone who has been threatened with death and bullets, 99% of them are false as fuck and scare tactics. Nothing happened, and nothing probably will.

However, again, we are Punjabi. We all have "Back." Sometimes we are the "Back." We have friends who make people think twice about fucking with us. The thing with these friends or cousins that we have for these instances is that the streets eventually take them. As young brown kids, we go to way too many funerals of young brothers who caught a bullet after they let them fly a few times. Unless you are involved in the streets, you have no business bringing them into your petty squabbles.

One thing I have learned is that your people are willing to help you when you are on defense. However, if you are looking for a problem, your closest friends will abandon you in times of conflict. Pay this mind, it is a great lesson.

We need to handle things the old way with fists. 1 moment of aggression and then put it all aside. Somewhere along the way we became too pussy to take a beating, and this is why we resorted to calling for help.

There is no shame in losing a fight. There is permanent

shame in hiding from one.

Close Call

So this one night buddy called me and found a girl who was on Tinder who was down to come out and drink with both of us. That was not really too out of the ordinary, especially in our culture. But what was out of the ordinary is that she was willing to do this with two guys she had never met, and on top of that, was willing to do so with someone she had just been talking to hours before.

Right then we should have known something was off.

However, I understand that the good Lord provides us with easy Women once in a while. I assumed this was just another one of those.

Buddy showed me pictures and she looked cute. Black girl mixed with a little something. *This is important*

We head out to pick her up and pull up outside her place to then bring her back to hours. Mind you, we like em THICC, but this once was just a bit THICC-er around the edges. Regardless, she was still good-enough to go.

We got acquainted on the ride home, she seemed nice enough.

Back to the place and started listening to music and having drinks. For the record we weren't expecting a tag team as it doesn't happen often. However, much crazier things have happened so there was a possibility. One drink turned to 4 plus shots.

It seemed as if she had taken more a liking to me. Buddy had recognized this and lays back. He's a good sport even though it's his introduction. I've been on the other side of that a couple times myself, so it was all good. I show the girl the rest of the house.

As soon as we get a bit of privacy we begin going at it. Doors are shut and after 3-4 minutes of foreplay, I guided her to give me domes. She agreed but was a weird one.

She basically would give me top for 5 seconds and then just stroke me for 2 minutes. It was a glorified hand job at best. I told her to get to it, thinking she was just warming me up, but nope. This went on for like 10.

I am extremely lucky that I am not able to finish quickly once I have had a few drinks. I am especially not easy to finish when someone else is pacing me. I can make myself finish in under 5. Someone else's hand, and I can be there all day. *This is also Important*

She tells me to finish on her chest but I just can't. God got me and protected me from myself.

We get dressed and go back downstairs. This is when things started to take a very weird turn.

The girl had a few more drinks, and stiff ones on that. She starts to lose her shit. To this day I have no idea what the fuck made her flip her switch but she got really aggressive. She began claiming shit like how a crew was coming over to rob us and shit. A bunch of back and forth arguing ensued, we knew she was full of shit, but then again in the world of the Internet, you never really know.

We told her to get the fuck out of the house, but she wouldn't leave without money to get home and then some. We managed to get her outside the door when she threw her phone on the ground in a fit of rage. She still wanted money. It was at this point we didn't really want to deal with bullshit so we closed the door on her and hung out wondering what the fuck had just happened.

An hour went by and we received a blocked number phone call. We assume it was her or someone who was trying to threaten us. To our astonishment, it was the cops. The girl had told them that we broke her phone and tried raping her.

We were fucking flabbergasted. At a complete loss for words. That was the first time anyone had accused me of something like that and it shook me to my core. Naturally we wanted nothing to do with it but the cop insisted that we come meet up him to clear it up.

We did so and explained our story. How this was a Tinder date that went to hell. Most of the time the word of 2 big brown guys against the word of 1 woman would not bode well. In this case however, given that she was way more drunk and speaking reckless, the cop believed us and didn't cause any further fuss about it.

Here's what went well for us. Not to be racist, but her being black and looking a little ratchet helped our cause. Again not to be prejudice, but if this was a blonde hair blue-eyed white girl, we'd be in some fucking trouble. Secondly, I couldn't Nut. This meant that none of my semen was on her body. I honestly think that this may have been the reason for the shitty domes. I mean she looked like she'd give the sloppy toppy no joke. But maybe she just wanted to give as little head as possible to make me nut and then black mail me or something. The third thing was we had a camera system to show how aggressive she was acting in my entry way. Not that the cops asked to see the footage, but that was something that covered us. Lastly, she got way to belligerent.

I thank the good Lord every day that this situation didn't turn into something ugly and drawn out. We knew we did nothing wrong, but in today's day and age people want to tear you down so you'd be getting fucked by people on platforms everywhere, without even knowing the truth. Reputations can be destroyed very easily through shit like this.

Moral of the story, in the internet age, don't be so quick to invite girls you don't know over to your house. I mean I won't let one bad experience shake me. But I would be lying to you if I told you these type of incidences didn't creep up in the smallest corner of my mind while I was meeting randoms.

Life isn't fair

Life isn't fair, and it never has been.

One time in Grade 12, senior year, of high school I decided to run for class president. I had absolutely zero interest in the job at the time. I also had zero experience. Upon applying, I was rejected. However, I could apply for school Treasurer. Again, I didn't have much an interest in the job, but I knew I was popular enough to win and make a joke of the system.

I was always a bit of an anti-establishment type of guy. I just wanted to see it burn.

What ensued in the weeks leading up to election day was the single biggest campaign run in the history of my High School. The race for presidency had taken a back seat.

We had printed hundreds of posters. Hundreds more than anyone else, presidential candidate or not. Every where you looked, you could see my mug on a poster. Everywhere in the school.

What I had, aside from charisma and the general support across the board, were the hinds. No "Hinds" had ever really run for something like that. Sure, brown kids had won and run these elections. But someone from our world; the world of Lincoln Navigators with rims, the world of parent's Mercedes in the parking lots, the world of Ed Hardy and Christian Audiger, was unheard to have a shot at doing this. My crew was willing to cause chaos and make more noise than any other campaign that had preceded before us.

This had gotten me into a lot of trouble. Certain people who supported us were ripping down the posters of those who ran against me. Personally, I did not believe in that at all. I did not need to play dirty. I knew I was going to win. I had then begun to have certain teachers hate on me. Information was leaked about how I was making a joke of it all, which I was. There were constant angles looking to disqualify me. One teacher had an issue with my poster. We didn't change it, my guys plastered those all over the outside of hi classroom. He called me in for a chat and explained how disrespectful that was. This was a teacher that I respected, so I felt bad.

I was told by members of staff to quit the race if I wasn't going to take the job seriously. I carried on and campaigned hard. It wasn't even going to be close, so long as I made it to election day.

The day came and the results were counted. Surprisingly, I was found to have lost. There was no possible way this could have happened. We had a class of 120ish and there was no way that I did not receive the lion's share of the 3 of us who ran.

A day later, a trusted teacher of mine leaked the news that the teachers were never going to allow me that position even if I had all the votes. Some of my votes were miscounted. Some were thrown out. Some I even heard were erased and scratched in another box. I don't have the evidence, but I do know in my heart that I had won. The staff made a judgment call on me and what I represented. They couldn't have me in office. To this day this is one of the biggest scandals in Cambie Secondary election history.

The point I am trying to make is that you can do everything right sometimes in life and still fail. Not to say that my campaign was pure or right, but I did everything by the book. It was my crew that pushed the envelope a bit too far. But at the end of the day, I love every one of those guys regardless because of how they tried to put one of our own on.

Regardless, sometimes life just isn't fair and this is something you are going to have to deal with. However, just because I got fucked over in that one instance doesn't mean that I would stop overall. Just a fact of life. Some people start off with more or less than you. Where you end up is up to you.

No matter where you are in life consider yourself to be God's favorite and run forward towards anything you want to accomplish. Quite simply, you ARE God's favorite, but so is everyone else.

Epilogue

By the time you have this in your hand and are reading this, it will be well into 2020. I decided to finish all the content of this book before the end of 2019. That's not because I believe in some bullshit like "leaving some woes behind" or "closing off a chapter and on to the next," even though ironically it is like that.

Part of this was to give me a deadline so I wouldn't keep putting it off. Part of this is that a do like a bit of poetic timing. Another part is because by the time I have the physical copies in my hand, we will probably be in mid-summer where I can start scheduling live readings.

I will definitely be doing Vancouver and Toronto. If any other place can get even 20-30 people out, I'd be more than happy to fly out. I'm not really doing this for any monetary value, I am blessed that I make more than enough running my business. I am however doing this for the sake of my own self-importance. Plus the bonus of meeting people who fuck with you on a certain level is just crazy to me.

I did this for the frustrated young kid out there who has a hard time with the ladies. I did this to show you my flaws and that fuck-ups are what lead to success. That eating shit over and over and over is what gives you the experience that you begin to pick up on the patterns of women. By no means am I an expert; I have just been in the game long enough. I am to game what Jared Dudley is to the Los Angeles Lakers; pretty shitty, but in the NBA regardless.

I also did this for the sake of the culture. To share the things that a young brown man goes through for the sake of getting laid. I apologize if any of the girls who had relations with me took any of this to heart, but in all honesty you're all grown fucking women, so quit that bullshit. This was also to show people who are not from our culture what it is like. Maybe we share similar struggles, but I can't speak on that. I can only speak from my perspective.

I appreciate every single one of you who took the time out to read this. I never thought I would have written a book in reality. This just kind of came together. I can't stress how grateful I am.

Thank You for allowing me to accomplish one more little thing in my life that feeds my ego. I can now tell new women that I have written a book. Bitches like interesting guys. Queens Love Them.

One Last thing, I let this project breathe for over 150 days after January 1st, 2020. The book was supposed to be finished by then. As much momentum as I had I decided to slow it down to focus on my real life and real career. Real, meaning in this context, as what makes me money. However, I still had few thoughts that I needed to get out. So I carried on and added more perspectives.

Once more, Thank You, and I look forward to what's next.

I am Humbled.